Good Grief!

A Holistic & Practical Approach to Healing Through Heartache

Be gentle with yourself along the way

With love,
Deborah

Deborah Edgar

Contents

Contents

For Jon

Thank you for showing up

and loving me so boldly and unconditionally.

I will love you

Forever and always.

Acknowledgment

To my sons, Joseph and Jacob: Without you, my life would be empty and dull. You are the greatest legacy I could possibly leave. We have traveled roads of adventure and turmoil together, and I wouldn't want to do it with anyone else. You have taught me so much about life, love and living authentically. You have cared for me in times of darkness and made me laugh so hard I cried. I love you both beyond measure, and I am insanely proud of you.

To my daughters-in-love, Kaitlyn and Katelyn: Thank you for loving my sons the way you do. Your unconditional and encouraging love for them fills my heart with intense joy. Thank you for loving them and all of my grandchildren the way you do. I love you.

To my grandchildren, this book is for you. Live with a spirit of adventure and hold tight to love in all its forms. Above all else, stay true to *yourself* and live with deep passion. I'm so proud of all of you, and I love you with a full heart.

To Roberta Damon, my therapist and dear friend: Without you, I would be lost. Words seem inadequate to describe your patience, compassion, gentleness and love that carried me through decades of unraveling into the light. Because of you, I am able to live authentically, with passion and zest and to love deeper than I ever imagined. I love you so much.

To my mentors: Valley Haggard, my writing coach; Stacy Wood, my life coach; Traci Ford, my health coach. The three of you have impacted my life in ways I will never be able to fully measure. Your compassion and nudging have helped me reach unimaginable heights. I'm the best I've ever been because of your belief in me. I thank you.

I would be remiss if I didn't thank my extended family and closest friends. I will not name them all here for fear of forgetting someone. I have been blessed my entire life to have the best friends anyone could ask for. You know who you are. You've stood by my side through the happiest and darkest days of my life. Each one of you has encouraged me to live the highest expression of myself, with deep love and compassion and the sharing of laughter and tears, and for that, I thank you.

carried me through decades of uncertainty into the light. Because of you I am able to live authentically with passion and zest and [illegible] than I ever imagined. I love you so much.

[illegible]

"Your pain is the breaking of the shell that encloses your understanding.

Even as the stone of the fruit must break that its heart may stand in the sun, so must you know pain.

And could you keep your heart in wonder at the daily miracles of your life, your pain would not seem less wondrous than your joy.

And you would accept the season of your heart, even as you have always accepted the season that passes over your fields."

Kahlil Gibran

The Paradox of Grief

Many years ago, I wrote this description of the grief I was experiencing:

"Grief: The painful distance between a life-changing event and the acceptance of its impact upon the rest of your life."

Grief sucks, and it is sacred. There is deep and dark pain as well as extraordinary beauty within its walls. It roars like a lion and is gentle as a lamb. It demands your attention then holds you at a distance. It appears as an unwanted guest, having its way until it becomes a welcoming friend. It is relentless and forgiving. There is no better analogy to better understand grief than the caterpillar who must shed itself to become a butterfly. So must we.

Throughout the healing process, two things can be experienced at the same time. We can be grateful and enraged. We can be certain about some things and uncertain about others. We can see a glimmer of hope one minute and dissolve into a puddle of despair the next. It's the beautiful paradox of grief itself that can be cleansing and healing, offering hope to the brokenhearted.

We are so beautifully fragile, living in a pain-avoidance culture that demands the heart-broken to "get up, be strong, and move on!" It's no wonder so many suffer in silence, turning to substance or drug abuse, rage or violence. There is no safe place to go with our heartache. We are encouraged and sometimes shamed into silence and isolation. It's easier for us to hide and pretend than to fight the demands of our culture.

There is grief inside of grief. The internal dialogue buried within our hurting hearts includes shame, guilt, and lack of confidence. We turn inward, where isolation and loneliness take on a life of its own. Our culture's demand that we grieve privately, in our own way, is perpetuated by the message, "Everyone grieves differently." We are left to our own devices to navigate the painful path of despair and heartache.

Perhaps a better approach would be to view grief as a journey - a sometimes cruel and painful web of ebb and flow, to and fro, one step forward and two steps back, towards acceptance. We must be gentle with ourselves and others as we navigate the uncharted waters of rebuilding our lives.

Transforming our heartache or grief is never linear. In fact, it's anything but. Countless books have been written about the linear path to healing. I believe the cultural message that healing is a destination to achieve is bullshit. I'm not certain it's even possible or advisable. I certainly don't believe it's healthy.

Instead, it may serve us well to view our healing process as a tapestry, something we gingerly and tenderly weave and hold sacred, with the anticipation of living the best life possible under our personal circumstances, as challenging as that may be. Our grief is not something to move on from. It's something to be carried forward gently and with reverence.

I know how hard it is to hold a broken heart tenderly and graciously, with the desire to transform the pain it holds in ways that allow for growth and peace. It requires a desire and a commitment wrapped in willingness, bravery and courage. It's not for the faint of heart. Certainly, understanding and compassion from others, as well as our faith, can help soothe our pain, but we must do the hard work of observing our internal dialog and embracing the hurts that have taken up residence in our organs, veins and, most importantly, our hearts. There is deep beauty and grace in acknowledging and sitting with our grief, as difficult as it may be.

I believe we can live full, happy and productive lives in spite of the grief we understandably make room for in our hearts. Loss is not something to "get over." It's something to accept and incorporate into a new life, lived authentically, with dreams and hopes fulfilled. We can learn to honor our memories and our experiences and carry them with us as we venture to create a new and different life.

Your life is worth living despite the pain you may be feeling right now. I want to encourage you to wrap your arms around your heartache and embrace it in healthy ways that will lead to authentic and productive living filled with moments of joy, beauty and celebration. It will take commitment, time well spent, self-compassion and soul care, but it's possible. I promise you it is.

My desire is that what I have learned along my journey towards healing will serve as a beacon of light to help encourage you along yours.

Be gentle with yourself along the way.

Unhinged

Throughout my 66 years, I've experienced a great deal of heartache, including physical, emotional and sexual abuse, two divorces, the death of cherished loved ones, an eating disorder, a miscarriage that led to a complete hysterectomy, a debilitating familial identity crisis, loss of direction, loss of jobs and relationships, and most recently the traumatic and sudden death of the love of my life. I've spent many years feeling overwhelmed, unsettled, lonely and isolated.

My confidence has been shaken to the core countless times, leaving me feeling unable to measure up or move forward, frozen in the grips of despair. As a dear friend recently suggested, most despair can be summed up in a single word: *Unhinged.*

My journey through profound sadness and heartache began as a little girl. I didn't know it at the time, but I was being groomed by a narcissistic mother and abusive stepfather to live with grief and depression as though it was the life source running through my veins.

I was born into my mother's third loveless marriage in 1957. When I was just three years old, she would leave that husband to pursue a life with a married man, who was also an alcoholic abuser. In an era of bobby socks and drive-ins, our life was filled with hidden emotional and physical abuse and the keeping of secrets that would protect our caretakers at the expense of everything.

When I look at pictures of myself as a little girl, I'm amazed at how happy I looked and how cute I was. I have baby pictures of myself throughout my house as a reminder of that sweet, innocent little girl who experienced abuse at the hands of those whose job it was to protect her. My happy, innocent face was a groomed prerequisite for hiding the abuse and never speaking of it.

When banished to my room as punishment, I found solace in books and journals. I was perfectly happy to quietly retrieve my little flashlight and my latest library book hidden beneath my mattress. I would pull the covers over my head, turn on my flashlight and read and write for hours. I could escape to a world that inspired me and offered hope for my future. Reading and writing would serve as the deepest and most impactful way for me to deal with my reality. I found comfort in journaling my experiences and feelings. It became the release I needed to block out the reality on the other side of my bedroom door.

At the tender age of 14, my only brother was burned to death in a tragic trucking accident at the age of 28. Not only was he my rock and salvation, he was my best friend. He had served as my protector against the harsh reality of emotional, physical and sexual abuse.

The night of his death, my stepfather firmly grabbed my elbow and led me outside, away from the family that had gathered to mourn. He forcefully put his pointing finger in my face and told me the consequences I would suffer if I shed another tear. I had been on the receiving end of his abuse for years. Although I trembled inside, I immediately put on a stiff upper lip.

I pushed my grief deep into the crevices of my soul. It found its way through my veins to harden my heart, act out in unspeakable ways and harvest resentment. From there, I carried grief, hurt and heartache into every relationship, both personally and professionally. Burying my pain took a tremendous toll in all areas of my life. I was an *unhinged* mess.

In my early 30s, while in my second marriage, I suffered a miscarriage in the fifth month of my pregnancy, resulting in a complete hysterectomy. I was devastated by the loss and the idea I could never have more children. I was reminded time after time by well-meaning people that I was "lucky to have children" and I "should be grateful." Yes, yes, I was grateful. But that didn't stop the *grief* I felt for the baby I miscarried or the ones I would never have.

I needed help to sort out the pain and agony I had buried for years. I was overwhelmed and exhausted by my past poor choices and those of others. My second marriage was in shambles, and I was in desperate need of guided healing. I knew it would take a special person to help me sort through, unravel and heal all the grief and confusion my soul contained.

I was fortunate to find the right therapist for me. It was a long and winding road, but with Roberta's guidance, compassion and care, we worked together over many years to transform my broken heart. I will forever be grateful for her gentle and compassionate guidance in helping me understand the magnitude of the abuse I had endured and the toll it had taken on my life and especially my Spirit.

Following several years of therapy and my second divorce, I was faced with more devastating and life-altering news. At the age of 45, I learned my father was not my biological father. This was a secret my parents had carried and held from me all of my life. To say that it threw me into another bout of darkness is an understatement. The magnitude of this life-changing event was unbearable at times. I was forced to begin the painful journey of facing the truth of my parentage and the impact of their lies upon my life. I was thrown into a real-life identity crisis.

My siblings were no longer my siblings, my grandmother, someone else's. I looked in the mirror and didn't recognize the face staring back at me. The harsh reality of DNA test results settled into my weary bones like a cancer with no cure. While the DNA results proved within 99% certainty that my father wasn't my father, it didn't provide evidence of who was. My mother's suggestion was that I simply believe, without question or evidence, that my stepfather was my biological father. Given I detested him and his abuse, I was not willing to accept her word, given she had lied to me my entire life. As a result of my insistence for evidence, my mother disowned and disinherited me in favor of her pristine reputation. We were estranged for the rest of her life.

I dedicated myself to unraveling. I allowed it to have its way with me. While it was painful, it was deeply cathartic and served a deeper purpose. I was grateful to have the foundation of previous healing work to help shore me up. Looking back, this was a gift that led me to explore the truth of who I am and who I wanted to be as I move through life.

I began to embrace my circumstances as an opportunity to begin again. I took a deep dive into *self*-development and devoured every book written by those who had traveled the path before me. There were many stumbling blocks along the way, and I continued to grapple with my sordid past and former poor choices, but I was determined.

I turned to my Creator for answers and solace. I found peace in building a new foundation of faith, one that gently held my broken pieces. I leaned into building a life that I felt was successful, peaceful and harmonious. I found myself to be a content and happy single person, living an authentic life filled with anticipation, longing and wonder. I finally understood the *spiritual* meaning of being "born again." I was enjoying the life I had built, one brick of foundation at a time.

Following the rebuilding and restoration of my life, and against many odds, I pursued a career in real estate, purchased my first home, and ultimately opened an independent real estate brokerage. I had accomplished something I could be proud of in spite of my rocky foundation. I had built anew.

And then, when least expected, I met Jon, the love of my life. In an instant, our lives changed upon meeting on a cold January morning. Over time, we thoughtfully and gently walked towards deep and passionate love. We took our time to commit ourselves loving one another unconditionally and forever. We locked arms and hearts to live a very happy and harmonious life. Individually, we had done the hard work of therapy and healing from past relationships, and we protected ourselves and our love, peace being our primary focus. Our mutual love exuded from us and we relished in sharing it with our families and friends. We shared almost five glorious years together before it was over in an instant.

While dancing with me and my grandchildren at my youngest son's wedding reception, Jon collapsed and died on the dance floor. It was a horrific tragedy that unfolded into a nightmare for all of us. Chaos erupted as my sons and other guests began CPR, trying to save his life. By the time first responders arrived, it was too late. It's still challenging to wrap our minds around the enormity of the loss of Jon's physical presence and certainly the way he died.

As a family, we have faced our challenges together. We have intentionally embraced this tragic event and have worked to transform it into a celebration of love. It hasn't been easy, but we have stood by one another through it all. Early on, we made a conscious decision to live love forward - in honor of Jon.

The initial shock and trauma of his death brought on medical issues, including severe memory loss, sleeplessness and inability to function. My sons and their wives took care of me for weeks as I found myself in a desperate fog of disbelief and despair. Looking back, I am grateful we have a built-in shock absorber that kicks in when our minds and hearts could possibly explode from trauma. That is a gift from our Creator, for certain.

As I gently made my way towards healing, I also made a conscious decision to observe my grief and that of others. I decided to track what worked for me - and what didn't. I literally watched my grief from a point of observation. I made progress with each step, even if some of those steps included missteps.

What I learned along the way has been life-changing. It has brought hope and inspiration to my soul. I've learned we are perfectly capable of reaching higher ground, seeking safe spaces, and encouraging the wounded towards authentic healing in the midst of darkness. We can learn to live joyful and authentic lives again and encourage others along the way.

I share my life experiences as a means to assure others that with grace, compassion and unconditional love, we can lift our consciousness towards true, authentic healing. No matter what you are experiencing, there is hope for the *unhinged.*

Life can be incredibly challenging and difficult. But, with a road map of sorts towards healing and with the desire for it, it can be embraced and lived beautifully. Let's walk this path together.

The Sacred Art of *Mourning* Rituals

It's 5:00 *am.* Eyes wide open, and there's no turning back. Pulling the covers over my head for another 30 minutes of restlessness sounds like the best option when I don't have the energy or desire to drag myself out of bed. Rest is elusive when you are tending a broken heart. It's an exhaustion no amount of sleep can cure.

Many mornings during my journey have been met with dread. Once my eyes popped open and reality hit, I would toss and turn, trying to convince myself that thirty more minutes would make all the difference. When it didn't, I would drag myself up, leaving my bed unmade. I'd head to the kitchen to make a cup of coffee, convincing myself it would "wake me up." I'd follow that with a sleeve of cookies, believing a little sugar couldn't possibly hurt anything. I'd open my phone, check for text messages, voicemails, and aimlessly scroll Facebook for anything I may have missed overnight. I motioned through all of it with resentment and indifference. I simply just wanted to go back to bed, pull the covers over, and wish the world and my reality away.

When I was a kid, I was required to make my bed the minute my feet hit the floor. I thought it was the most ridiculous thing. After all, I was just going to crawl back in at the end of the night. This required routine was one of a long list of "rules" in our household that I grew to resent. All of our rules centered around the number ten. Ten minutes to shower, ten minutes to talk on the phone. Curfew was 10 pm. Ten this, ten that. To this day, the number 10 makes me cringe. I found it humorous and insightful when I signed up for my first writing workshop with Valley, my writing coach. It was appropriately called "Life in 10 Minutes." The irony was not lost.

Over the years, with the guidance of trusted life coaches, I've discovered making my bed serves as a metaphor. I can start my day haphazardly, with no care, or I can start it with a little order. The rest of the day may be barely manageable, but making my bed and following a morning ritual is within my control. I've also learned it empowers me to keep going, no matter how I'm *feeling.*

With patience and compassion, I've committed to putting the tender care of my soul above all else. I've created a morning routine that serves my healing and has become sacred. When I wake, I get up. It's not unusual for me to "rise and shine" at o'dark 30. Once my bed is made, I pour a large glass of water and drink it before I have my *required, perfectly made* cup of java.

That's followed by reading or listening to something uplifting or encouraging. I usually start with Stacy Wood's book, "*Own Your Journey*." It is a daily dose of insightful guidance to create a desired path to living authentically. Next, I honor my temple. I get moving. If I don't go to the gym or take a long walk, I pull up a session on SilverSneakers (it's free to many) and get my body moving. I've been known to dance in the kitchen at 6 am. I'm then ready to go about my day, taking care of that which is required. You know, the *necessities* of life.

Before you give your undivided attention to the ticker-tape excuses in your head about how you have kids to feed, emails to check, or the need to finish the last episode of *This is Us* that you fell asleep to last night, please hear me out. We all have a few minutes we can carve out at the beginning of our day. Quite frankly, the minute you open your eyes, you can claim the first thirty minutes as sacredly yours. Make a promise to yourself. No interruptions. No interference. Just you and your deepest desires to lean into. Is it always easy? Oh, hell no. Do I still grab that sleeve of cookies on occasion or slide back under the covers? Of course. In fact, just this morning, I had the most delicious chocolate-covered almonds for breakfast.

Be gentle with yourself as you begin to contemplate the day you desire. Start by creating a short list of things you can and will accomplish. Take your time to explore new things, switch things up and find your rhythm. Once you have your list, commit to starting your day a few minutes early. Just a few. Claim this time for yourself. Once you begin to achieve even the simplest of your heart's desires, you will look back upon the day with a sense of accomplishment.

And for the love of all things holy and sacred, do not open your phone or your laptop or turn on the TV before you complete your morning ritual! Once you do, you are sucked into the vortex. We all know what happens when we try to convince ourselves that the care of our soul can just as easily be accomplished after we watch the news or scroll social media for hours. Let's stop fooling ourselves. Our healing depends upon it.

A mourning ritual can help provide a road map to healing a broken heart. When all else seems lost, you can begin to trust in your own power and believe in the most important foundation - *your well-being*. Before you know it, you will be leaning into your transformation, one little sacred step at a time.

Honor Your Temple

I've always resented gym rats. I suppose deep down, I'm jealous of them. All that dedication and determination. The thought of it makes me roll my eyes and reach for another donut. I've started countless exercise classes, joined many gyms in January and vowed eternal commitment to something I knew I wasn't going to do. I always end up feeling like a quitter, making new promises every day and faltering on most.

When we are heartbroken, our energy goes to getting out of bed and brushing our teeth. I've spent many days wearing the same clothes and convincing myself that a shower every three days would suffice. We simply don't have the energy to think about exercise or drink more water, much less do it!

Through my teens and into my early twenties, I was obsessed with my weight and body image. It partly stemmed from my mother's constant negative remarks about my looks. She would put her finger up to my face and declare, "You need to do something about that blemish," or "I think you've gained a little weight, you might want to limit your portions." The diagnosis of bulimia or anorexia was not a "thing" in my early adult years, but I'm pretty sure it would be my diagnosis if I was still suffering with the same symptoms today.

Through therapy, I was able to heal that within myself that placed unhealthy value on my looks or the numbers on a scale. Still, taking care of my body continues to include a daily dose of far-reaching determination. I've learned to soften the demands I place on myself. I've faced the reality that I'm not going to get up at 6 am to attend a Zumba class, nor am I likely to drink as much water as is recommended.

Over time, I have reframed my thoughts about exercise and nutrition. I now refer to it as "Honoring My Temple." There is something sacred about loving your body back to health, one gentle step at a time. And there is something even more sacred about learning the difference between self care and soul care, both of which are important. I've learned to focus on the latter for my Spirit's sake. For me, *self* care looks like exercise for the sake of the scale, manicures and pedicures, massages and the like. *Soul* care goes deeper. It's the honoring of the temple from inside, with loving care and desire to be in optimal emotional and physical health.

Sadly, many of us have been convinced through generations that the soulful care of ourselves is selfish. This is another dangerous and sad commentary we have to fight within ourselves to overcome. It's not easy to turn the tide on these messages that harvest lack of self-worth, self-esteem, confidence and strength. We can, however, take gentle, loving and compassionate steps towards healing this belief, one baby step at a time.

About three months prior to Jon's death, I did what millions of other people do at the flip of a calendar year. I joined the local Y and hired a trainer. I had the good fortune of signing up with a delightful trainer by the name of Traci. She made it clear to me she was not interested in how much weight I wanted to lose or how my clothes fit. She was interested in my overall health. We began a journey together that would set me on track to be in the best health I've ever experienced. We took a holistic approach to healing through…drum roll….exercise!

And then, just four months later, my Tsunami hit. I texted Traci with the news of Jon's sudden death. Her response was short yet meaningful. "I will be here when you are ready. Don't forget to breathe." Over the next few months, she would send me short, encouraging messages. "Don't forget to move your body." "I'm here when you are ready."

It would be several months before following Jon's death that I would get back to our training sessions, but I believe it helped transform my ravaged soul. I would show up to our sessions in tears, sobbing as she lovingly yet firmly said, "You can cry all you want, but pick up those weights." And so I did.

Today, I am in the best physical shape I've ever enjoyed in my life. I'm stronger than I've ever been. I look forward to moving my body, and I've learned the value of a deep breath, something I now crave and seek daily. I've learned how my body works and why I want to strengthen certain muscles. I've learned the value of having strong bones, and I'm stronger mentally and physically. Most importantly, I simply feel better.

You don't have to join a gym or hire a trainer. Start with something simple. Drink an extra glass of water a day. Take a walk or a gentle yoga class. Schedule a physical. Take a nap.

Yes, take a nap. The restoration of your mind and body is vital when you are tending a bleeding heart.

Don't overwhelm yourself with unachievable goals. Make a list of simple things you believe you can achieve every day towards the care of your Temple. After all, it carries precious cargo!

Home Is Where The Heart Is

When you are rebuilding your life, regardless of the reason, it's important to create a sanctuary of respite for yourself. As Maya Angelou wrote, "The ache for home lives in all of us. The safe place where we can go as we are and not be questioned."

Of course, it's important on a spiritual level that we find a metaphorical home in our hearts, minds, and spirits, where peace beyond understanding resides. But our physical home, our personal space, is equally important. While you may not have the resources to move or redecorate, you can create a loving, peaceful, harmonious and safe space for yourself.

My home has become my sanctuary. It's a clear and direct reflection of my personality and what my soul needs to feel comforted, warm and secure. It's an eclectic and perfect combination of mismatches I've created over many years. I affectionately refer to it as my "flea market house."

When Jon died, I had to make the heart-wrenching decision to move out of the home that we had built side by side over four years prior to his death. It was our home, but it wasn't my house. In an instant, it belonged to others.

I was fortunate to be able to move back to the house I owned prior to meeting Jon, but it no longer felt like home. It did, however, serve as a clean slate for me to transform it into a sanctuary where I could be comforted in my grief. It also served as a reminder that I could start over and be okay. It is now a mirrored reflection of my personal taste and has become my lighthouse, no matter what storm I may be facing.

During my transition, I became acutely aware that I like to collect things. It was a challenging awareness, given everything I touch becomes sentimental or something "I may need later." When I realized just how much space and time healing requires, it became very clear to me that "stuff" takes up its own time and energy, and I became determined to do something about it.

I embraced the overwhelm of it all one drawer or closet at a time. Then I moved to the bigger spaces – like the garage, a storage unit I didn't need and an office I didn't use. Literally emptying one drawer at a time provided space and a deep breath that I didn't realize the clutter was stealing.

I added fresh flowers weekly. I stacked books on my coffee table, whether I read them or not. Seeing them there brought me comfort. I placed throw blankets on every bed and chair, making it cozy and comfortable for when I needed to curl up in a fetal position and have my down and dirty ugly cry.

While I've always had a roof over my head, and for that, I'm grateful, there have been times in my life when I felt homeless. I'm talking about homelessness of the heart. Grief does that. Change does that. Turmoil does that. We are left to feel homeless in our hearts when our lives are in shambles, turned upside down, inside out. It's innate within us to want to feel protected, safe, secure and peaceful. When that is interrupted, we can be left with a sense of unease and emptiness.

Our homes can offer refuge as we navigate the maze of healing our hearts. If you don't have a feeling of comfort where you are planted right now, I want to encourage you to make small changes that will eventually lead to your heart feeling more at home.

Over time, you will have created a cherished and safe sanctuary for yourself, one that will serve as a welcoming space to honor your heart's desires.

It Can Be Brutal Out There

Contrary to popular belief, it's not the acknowledgment and embracing of our emotions that may kill us, but the dismissal of them that just might.

We don't have to venture too far past our front doors to realize our culture's need to avoid emotional pain at all costs. We are encouraged to "move on" from grief as quickly as it comes, and quite frankly, we are often shamed if we don't. We hide our heartache or numb it and pretend we are okay, all for the sake of the American way. It's simply not healthy. We can and must do a better job of acknowledging and comforting our collective broken hearts.

In conversations with people who are grieving, one of the main topics they share is how hurtful and insensitive others can be when responding to their grief. We seem to have a ready-made list of platitudes that are used to dismiss feelings, often disguised as well-meaning words of comfort. While these passed-down, watered-down clichés may be intended for good, oftentimes, they result in more heartache to those already suffering enough. If we are bent towards dismissing our own pain, certainly, we are quick to dismiss it in others.

Worse yet, if we are shamed into believing we "should be……better, stronger, further along…." we may find ourselves more deeply burdened by the idea we simply aren't measuring up in some way. It's no wonder we suffer in silence. The world turns us away, so we turn inward, where it feels safer.

Unfortunately, we have an uphill battle in front of us to change our culture's dismissive attitude towards emotional pain. It will take a lot of education and patience to turn the tide to understand words really do matter and that our pain is deserving of acknowledgement and deep care. My voiced concerns about this issue have been dismissed time and again by people responding, "Deborah, don't be so hard on people; they mean well."

Recently, a woman shared with me that she thought my idea of trying to change our culture's course on this topic was selfish of me. She went on to say that I should just dismiss what people say to people who are in pain as "their attempt to help." Another woman suggested, "I guess before it's over, no one will say anything to someone who is hurting for fear of being judged for it."

I found these responses interesting. I contemplated both and checked my ego. I don't believe it's selfish or inconsiderate to suggest we can raise the bar on consciousness. Of course, we will falter. Of course, I will say ridiculous and hurtful things at times, and so will you. But can't we collectively agree we can do better and take even small steps towards a collective effort? I believe we can.

There is no doubt most people "mean well" when responding to grief, but we can reach for higher ground, can't we? As Maya Angelou reminds us, "When you know better, you DO better." I believe we can work together to learn how to uplift, empower and bring comfort to one another in words and deeds.

It is my hope that shedding light on some of these messages will lead us to think before we speak. We can learn to offer uplifting, loving and sincere words of comfort to those whose hearts are breaking, rather than rely on generational clichés that push the hurting back under metaphoric bed covers into isolation or deep depression.

Following Jon's death, if one more person told me he was "in a better place," I thought my head might spin around three times and green vile would project out of my mouth - exorcist style. I felt there was no better place for him to be than by my side. The notion that he was now in a "better place" didn't bring comfort to the void of him not being present, continuing to share the life we considered to be *heaven on earth*. I would have preferred to hear, "Please tell me about the relationship you and Jon shared. I'd love to hear more about it."

When I had a miscarriage, people said to me, "Well, you are lucky to have your two sons." "You are young, you can try again." Little did they know, I couldn't. My pain was dismissed under the cold blanket of the demand to *feel* grateful. I would have preferred to hear, "My heart is aching with yours." Or simply, "I'm so sorry."

One day, when I was sobbing over my second divorce, my mother said to me, "Why are you crying? I thought this is what you wanted." No. It wasn't what I "wanted." It's what I needed to do for the survival of my soul. No one gets married with the desire to get divorced. Regardless of the fact it was my decision, my dreams were shattered, and my life was in shambles. Again, my feelings were dismissed under the guise of it being my own life-changing decision. I would have preferred to hear, "Divorce is disappointing and life-altering. Cry all you want."

At a funeral I attended shortly following Jon's, an acquaintance approached me. "Oh my God, I heard what happened to you. I heard Jon was a really nice man. I hope you know how lucky you were." I looked at her in disbelief, but it didn't stop her. "I wish I could meet a man like that. There just aren't any good ones out there." She continued, "Don't worry, you are young; you will meet someone else. And when you do, ask him if he has a brother. I'm looking for a man." I could not get away from this person fast enough. Thankfully, another mutual friend was standing beside me. She gently touched my elbow as if to guide me. She whispered, "Would you like to help me find the restroom?" "Yes, yes I would," I responded with relief. As we walked away, my friend said, "Oh my God. What the absolute hell?" I sobbed all the way to my car.

Following Jon's death, I was often told, "I hope you know how *lucky* you were." Yes. Of course, we both knew how lucky *we* were. We welcomed one another into our lives with open arms. We created a life together that was precious and cherished. I was fortunate, no question. But I was also lost, confused, lonely and in turmoil following his death. Again, I retreated into feeling that perhaps gratefulness and feeling "lucky" should overshadow my real feelings of desperation. No real transformation can come from that.

A couple of years ago I returned to an oceanside town where Jon and I vacationed the previous year. I went to one of the restaurants we enjoyed and reintroduced myself to the bartender that had served us the year prior. I shared with her that Jon had died. She shared with me that her mother had died the same month he did and that she was going through a divorce following 15 years of marriage. She went on to share that her husband had asked one too many times in a few months following her loss, "When are you going to get over your mother's death?" "We need to get on with our lives." She filed for divorce. I'm sure his dismissal of her feelings didn't start with the death of her mother, but it was the nail in the coffin of their marriage. I'm certain she would have preferred to hear, "We will get through this together, no matter how long it takes."

My friend Michele has called me countless times to share when her heart has been stabbed by well-meaning yet insensitive remarks. Shortly following the tragic death of her husband, whom she cherished and cared for through the cruel disease of ALS, people began asking, "When are you going to take off your rings and start dating again?" "You are young, you will meet someone else." She described these comments as a dagger to her already wounded heart. Hearing these thoughtless comments would understandably send her into a tailspin of debilitating days. I'm pretty sure she would have preferred to hear, "Your rings are lovely; they are a beautiful symbol of your undying and eternal love."

When my son's house burned down several years ago, I recall people saying, "Thank God no one was hurt or died." Of course, we were thankful no one was hurt or dead. The rest of his losses seemed to be dismissed under the global umbrella of what he should be grateful for. In an instant, my son and his family, including five children, lost everything they owned in a matter of minutes.

When the Red Cross volunteer handed my son seven toothbrushes in a small, plastic bag, as we stood amidst the smoldering embers of treasures, he looked at me and said, "Mom, I didn't even think about the fact that we don't have toothbrushes." In that moment, he may not have been able to *simply* be grateful no one was hurt or dead. He was forced to focus on rebuilding their entire life - one toothbrush at a time.

It was my son who taught me that it would be helpful if people would show up months or even years following a tragedy. He recalled people showing up with clothes, dishes, food, etc., immediately following his house fire. While he was overwhelmed with gratitude, he also logistically didn't have a place to store it all. He was then faced with the additional burden of managing household goods while sorting out temporary housing for his family. Now, when he hears people requesting help for others in similar situations, he suggests allowing them space and time to start to rebuild. They will need food, household items and money a year from now as well.

The same holds true for those going through the loss of a loved one, a divorce, or any other tragedy. Most of us show up at the onset of an event. We take food, send cards, and deliver flowers. Then, shortly thereafter, the doors darken, the flowers wither, and the bereaved are left to "get on with it." Perhaps we could start a trend to show up months or even years following a heart-altering moment, dinner in hand.

When my youngest son returned from a harrowing experience in Afghanistan, there is no doubt I said hurtful, dismissive things to him. While he was going through the unspeakable turmoil of putting his life back together, I simply wanted him to "get back to normal."

Over time, and through loving and respectful, yet difficult, conversations, I learned how I was causing him additional heartache. I realized my fear of losing him to despair was resulting in my dismissing his feelings. I'm sure he would have preferred I say, "I can't possibly understand what you have gone through or know your pain. I am here for you, as your mom and friend, to walk beside you as you take this journey towards healing."

If someone says something that feels insensitive to you, take a deep breath and remind yourself it's not personal. It's most likely a matter of them not knowing what to say that will be helpful or repeating memorized platitudes that have been passed down generation to generation. Or, it may be their own pain and fear speaking.

I'm often reminded that people who are grieving don't really want to be reminded of their strength. They would rather their tenderness and fragility be recognized. That alone would give them a welcome relief and the ability to begin to move more gently and purposefully into their innate strength.

The dismissing of others' emotions is oftentimes what we do to deflect our own pain and fears. Too often, we just want others to feel better, so we don't have to deal with their pain, or ours. I get it, but we must do better. Very well-meaning people simply don't know what to say and certainly aren't aware of how deeply words can sting. Awareness and willingness is key to changing our culture's dismissive nature.

Over time, I've learned *words matter.* It's not an easy path to maneuver, but I believe we can all do a better job of choosing our words carefully and gently. I've stumbled along the way, and I know it's not an easy task, but I believe it's necessary.

As my journey has progressed, I've grown strong enough to share with others how some of their responses contribute to my hurting heart. As an example, when someone says, "He's in a better place," I respond, "I appreciate your belief. However, we shared heaven *here on earth.* I simply want him to be *here.* In my heart, there is no better place than that." It hasn't always been easy to have those conversations, but I've learned to do it with love and compassion and a desire to raise the collective bar of consciousness.

It is absolutely not selfish to kindly tell people how you feel and what is helpful…or not. Together, we can learn to be more comfortable in asking for our needs to be met, all the while embracing compassion and kindness in all its forms.

Most people truly mean well. Don't allow the less thoughtful remarks to take root in your grieving heart.

Lean Into Your Trusted Tribe

We are seldom prepared when heartache strikes. I've been blessed and fortunate over my lifetime to build a tribe of family and friends I can rely upon. They are on standby for the good, bad and ugly. Over time, these treasured relationships have become steadfast foundations through unsteady times. I know the people I can count on at any given moment. And they know they can count on me.

My friend Melissa and I have a code word between us. If we are having a challenging day, we know to call or text each other with one simple word, "Corner." We came up with our code word the day after we had reached out to each other in despair. She was grieving the loss of her son, and I was reliving the pain of Jon's death.

We decided to meet that evening at a little dive bar in our neighborhood. The Corner is the perfect gathering spot for grabbing a burger and a beer. We needed both. What we didn't know is that they have a jukebox! Before we knew it, we were cashing our ones for quarters, delighting in what songs we wanted to hear. We created a dance floor on the front porch, dancing our sorrows away and asking others to join in. We laughed, cried and laughed some more. Now, if either of us sends the quick one-word message of "Corner," we know we are meeting at 6 pm. No questions or excuses. We know it's *that* important. And we know it's something we can count on.

My friend Susan and I text frequently. We've been friends for many years, and over the past two, we have shared the path of profound grief. We seldom actually talk over the phone. However, if I get a text message from her asking if I can talk for a few minutes, I drop everything and dial her number. She does the same for me. That's essentially our code for "I need you *now*!"

Having known each other for more then three decades, my friend, Matthew, and I have been witness to many of one another's celebrations and pitfalls. We have ebbed and flowed through many years, but over the past few, we reconnected in a powerful, thoughtful and consistent way. We have weekly conversations about our lives, our hopes and dreams, and our deepest desires. I aptly named our conversations "Mondays With Matthew." Just recently, we made an agreement to hold each other accountable for the way we talk about ourselves. We both suffer from the torturous habit of negating our worth. Now sealed by a pinky promise, we know we can depend on each other in an authentic, uplifting way, and our friendship has deepened as a result.

Relationships are vital when tending a healing heart. I highly recommend you write down a list of everyone you consider to be your Trusted Tribe. Call them and establish a code word between you. People love to feel needed, and they prefer when someone tells them what they can do to help versus having to guess or getting it wrong. By establishing an agreement now, you have already taken a major step towards engaging with one another to help carry the burden of heartache towards authentic healing.

To those who want to help someone who is grieving, I offer this. I often hear people tell the suffering, "Let me know *if* you need anything." Trust me, 9 out 10 people are *not* going to tell you what they need. First, they are *grieving*! They have no idea what they need at the moment. They can barely put one foot in front of the other and are most likely living in the fog of overwhelm. They will generally answer, "Thanks, but I'm okay." That's bullshit. They are not okay.

I suggest you simply show up and do something. Cut their grass. Deliver dinner to them. Tell them you are sending someone to clean their house. Call them for a shopping list. Tell them you are picking up their two-year-old for a play date on Saturday. Pick something helpful and show up and do it. Trust me, it's one of the greatest gifts you can bestow upon someone who is existing in the fog of grief. The old adage, "Actions speak louder than words," certainly applies when considering what to do for someone else. Just do something.

As The World Turns

I'm not talking soap operas here.

When your heart is in shambles, it's hard to imagine how the rest of the world continues to carry on as though nothing has happened. While your world is shattered into a million pieces, and you don't know how you are going to make it through the next hour, it seems everything and everyone else continues on as usual. It's human nature to wonder how the world can keep spinning when yours has imploded.

One of the best decisions I made after Jon's death was to stop watching the news. As I had my own tsunami unfolding, I simply couldn't bear the weight of bleak and devastating news accounts. While I had always believed it was my moral obligation to know what was going on in the world outside mine, I had begun to realize the weight of it upon my shoulders. I simply couldn't bear my own grief and that of the world's at the same time.

In hindsight, I had been a news junky. It wasn't uncommon for me to have the news blaring in the background as I drove, worked, exercised or rested. It empowered me in some way to feel that I was "informed." The truth is, the news doesn't empower us. It disempowers us. It provides a reason to metaphorically crawl back under the covers where it's safe and warm, where we can escape the madness. And, sadly, it numbs us in ways we don't even notice.

Having weaned myself away from the constant barrage of bad news, I can say my life is simpler, more enjoyable, less stressed and certainly more peaceful as a result of not hearing dreadful news accounts every day, all day.

If I want to know what the weather is, I look outside. If I want to know what the idiots in Washington are doing, I watch the ticker tape at the gym. Nothing really changes. It's the same story with a different headline - the story of the demise of our world and the message we are powerless against it. I often wonder what would happen if we stopped watching and listening and simply turned our attention to tending to the business of healing our own hearts and those around us. Wouldn't that help soften, if not solve, at least some of our collective heartache?

By limiting the news, I don't feel overwhelmed by things I can't control. I no longer get angry or shout vulgarities at the disgraceful acts people commit against one another. And, somehow, I don't miss the *Breaking News*. Believe me when I tell you - if there is something I need to know, someone will tell me. People love to share.

Don't get me wrong. I'm still a firm believer that we need to have a decent understanding of what's going on in the world outside our walls. It helps prepare us for what's coming our way and keeps our compassion in check. I'm simply saying that watching the news morning, noon, and night is a time and energy suck. Like it literally sucks the life out of ours.

While the world keeps turning while yours has imploded, consider taking a break from the news. Use that time to look within, to soothe your aching bones and tired soul. Read. Write. Seek Grace for yourself, watch a movie, take a walk, talk to a friend. Or take a nap. But, for the love of all things, tune out the madness. Yours is enough to endure for now.

Time Heals All Wounds And Other Ridiculous Notions

Let's get real. We are barraged with ludicrous and ridiculous notions about life and how to manage through it. I could write a separate book on this topic. For now, let's talk about a few that directly impact our hurting hearts and authentic healing.

Time Heals All Wounds

When I hear the sentiment, "Time heals all wounds," espoused as truth along with other cultural cliches that don't make sense, I want to shout from rooftop: "Please, stop the madness!"

Contrary to popular belief, time *does not* heal all wounds. That's ludicrous. The only thing time does is pass. It is what we choose to do with time that ultimately matters. We can use it wisely, or we can waste it. The choice is ours.

While it may be true that our pain eases over time, true healing requires endless effort. It's not something that magically happens with the passage of time. With tender care, our pain softens, and we learn to live with it differently.

It no longer feels like a huge boulder sitting in the middle of our chest, gripping our breath every waking moment. Instead, it becomes a pebble, a reminder that we have loved, a reminder that we carry forward with gentleness and grace.

While studying for my certification to become a holistic life coach, I was given an exercise in time awareness. This particular exercise is designed to debunk the myth that there "aren't enough hours in the day," as we often murmur as we scramble through our days. I was guided to account for every thirty minutes of my day. Every single minute, in thirty-minute increments. Yikes.

I was astounded. Did I really want to record that I had spent the last hour scrolling social media, learning what total strangers ate for dinner last night? Did I want to record that I could feel my blood pressure rise as I spent God knows how many minutes writing several replies and deleting them all in response to some dude I don't even know as he espoused I'm likely going to hell because I'm divorced? Did I want to record that I was spending valuable time scrolling to see if someone had liked a previous post? Did I want to admit in writing that I spent all this time doing *nothing* while convincing myself I didn't have time to exercise? No. No, I did not. The result of this exercise was like cold water in my face. I could no longer ignore the reality of how I was wasting precious time.

Worse yet, I was feeling inadequate, worthless and lazy. The truth is, I was not managing *myself* well. Time was passing as time does. It was not healing my wounds. It was not achieving anything worthwhile. It was being wasted. And I was the one wasting it. With awareness, I made a conscious decision to stop wasting so much time. I became acutely aware of my poor choices, and things started to happen. Like finishing this book! Pure, determined, peaceful energy and action is the force behind making time work best for us, thirty minutes at a time.

What Doesn't Kill You Makes You Stronger

When someone tells me, "What doesn't kill you makes you stronger," I think I may fall over dead from the dagger. I really don't need to be "stronger." I've had to be "strong" all my freaking life. I'd prefer if someone sees my gaping wound and tells me they see my fragility and vulnerability, all the while encouraging me that I will live through it. I need to hear that it's okay to feel like my pain is going to kill me and that with time well spent, it will be transformed or healed, and it won't feel like a continuously oozing bullet wound that just might take my life. I don't want this pain to be swept under the rug or be dismissed by spiritual or emotional bypassers intent on suggesting I just need to be "strong" to endure it. No, I'm *wounded* right now. I'd prefer to believe my vulnerability and desire to heal will carry me through it, one painful step at a time. Let's talk about *that.*

Things Can Always Be Worse

A dear friend of mine recently told me that when she has shared some of her heartache with loved ones, they responded, "Well, things can always be worse." This is a woman who lives a "picture-perfect" lifestyle from the outside. She numbs her pain with drugs as a result of it being dismissed under the umbrella of "things can always be worse." Her pain is buried beneath the idea she should simply be grateful for the life she's living. Sadly, we tend to shut down pain in others as a way of dismissing our calling to really hear or see it. We should never dismiss pain in another by suggesting "things can always be worse." When we are in pain, we deserve it to be acknowledged, not shunned or shamed into silence. Worse yet, we should never dismiss our own pain in favor of thinking, "It could always be worse."

Everything Happens for A Reason

I can't begin to count the number of times people have said to me, "Well, everything happens for a reason." It's usually just after a catastrophic life event has occurred. It's generally followed with, "We may never know the reason, but there is one." And then, the real whammy comes. "It's not ours to question." Wait. What?

If the current pain I may be experiencing right now isn't enough, now I'm pondering the mysterious, deep, insightful "reason" I was abused as a child, my spouse took a lover, or the love of my life dropped dead in front of me without warning. Well, thanks, but I'd rather not. I'd rather believe that sometimes, "Shit Happens."

I've experienced enough heartache in my life to be quite comfortable in saying, "No! Not everything happens for some mystical, divinely appointed reason." I've been challenged many times by people who firmly believe the opposite. And that's okay. I realize the stronghold this belief has on our culture, and I also realize the white-knucked response to holding on to this idea.

We all want to believe that everything happens for an understandable purpose or reason. Somehow, this platitude is meant to magically help make sense of the nonsensical. But, the burden of reason does not belong to the brokenhearted. It belongs to the Universe, something that we can't always understand or make sense of. Bearing our grief is challenging enough without feeling the need to examine a deep, unknown, mythical reason for it or the suggestion we should never question it. Sheesh.

God Will Never Put More on Your Shoulders Than You Can Bear

Really? First, I'm not a believer in God orchestrating *everything.* That simply doesn't make sense to me. I prefer to believe that Life happens and our faith in something greater than ourselves will bring us comfort as we maneuver through the maze of all of its challenges. Maybe I'm wrong, and God is orchestrating every single little thing that happens in our life at any given moment. Alternatively, I prefer to believe God is far too busy comforting our pain rather than causing it.

One of my favorite authors, Jeff Brown, recently shared this about the subject:

"God does not give you more than you can handle. Really? I get that we stay stuff like this because we don't know what else to say or because we think it actually helps. We don't want people to give up. We want them to keep on fighting to stay alive. But, honestly, it doesn't help. Few survivalist mantras do. Because there is more to life than survival at all costs. There is more to life than armoring up and toughing it out in the heart of our suffering. There is also something to be said for healing our way to wholeness. For meeting each other in our woundedness. For embracing the possibility that our trauma is actually a lot more than we can handle. So, next time you feel tempted to tell a trauma survivor, 'God does not give you more than you can handle,' try this instead: Something tragic has happened. You should not have to handle it alone. How can I help you to grieve and to heal? Remind them that God is a soft place to land. Remind them that God is compassion in human form."

I agree and believe with Jeff. He said it way better than I ever could. I love his term "survivalist mantras." It perfectly sums up that which is used to shut down our emotions and encourage us to "buck up, be strong and move on."

In fact, if you add the phantom sentence, "So, please move on," to the end of each of the examples given above, you will find it pretty much sums up how these notions contribute to shutting down our emotions. "Everything happens for a reason.....*so please move on.*" "What doesn't kill you makes you stronger....*so please move on.*"

With awareness and willingness, we can change the way we respond to grief, and we can turn the tide from spiritual and emotional bypassing to embracing the difficult and challenging path to true transformation.

I encourage you to be aware of how some of these messages can negatively impact you, your well-being and especially your healing. Emotional bypassing can drain your energy.

When you are healing, energy is your most important commodity. Don't let anyone steal it from you in the form of ridiculous notions.

Grab Hold of Your Faith or Explore a New One

Heartache and disappointment can rattle our faith. Nothing can shake it deeper than tragedy, abuse, deep confusion or a broken heart. Just when we may think we are on solid ground, an emotional earthquake hits and rattles us off our faithful foundation.

I don't believe the world is going to turn on its axis or burst into flames if we color outside the lines of our ancestral religious doctrines. When I was going through a serious identity crisis in my 40s, I was served a crisis of faith as a side dish. I had learned through a casual conversation with my father's sister that he was not my biological father. A simple suggestion that I wasn't his daughter because no one else in the family had blonde hair was enough to start a firestorm of uncovering lies that would change my life forever. It was a family secret that had been held from me all my life. It turned everything I believed to be true upside down and inside out. I truly didn't know who I was. I was forced to rebuild my identity and my faith in God.

I grew up in a household that touted the Bible and Christianity as truth, all the while covered by a blanket of keeping secrets and whispering half-truths behind closed doors. As I questioned a God who would allow my parents to drive to church with whiskey sours in hand, followed by emotional and physical beatings following Sunday dinner, my faith in Christianity and my belief in God faltered.

When I made an appointment at the age of 15 with our minister to tell him of the abuse at the hands of my parents, he shook his head and declared without question, "You certainly seem to have a vivid imagination." "What you are telling me cannot possibly be true." "Your parents would never behave in the manner you are describing."

I left his office dripping in shame and regret. If my trusted minister would not believe me, who would? I was reminded of when my stepfather told my mother that I was lying when I had confided in her that he had sexually abused me. She had also dismissed me as having a vivid imagination and a tendency to create lies to splinter and divide.

I began to question my own judgment and how God could possibly allow this, given the teaching from the pulpit that He orchestrates *everything*. I knew I needed to find comfort in an alternative Higher Being – one that was loving, compassionate and *knew* my heart.

During one of the darkest moments within my identity crisis, I screamed out to the heavens and asked that I be shown some semblance of a graceful, universal, loving, and understanding Being. On my knees, I asked for an undeniable sign for my future. I was in dire emotional pain, and my life depended on it. I was guided by that small, still voice we all have within us to retrieve my Bible and randomly open it. After shuffling through a few closets and drawers and bookshelves to find it, there it was on a bottom shelf. The New Believer's Bible. I randomly opened it. A particular verse stood out as though it was highlighted in bold, just for me:

Jeremiah 29:11-14. "For I know the plans I have for you. Plans to prosper you and not to harm you. Plans to give you hope and a future. Then you will call on me and come and pray to me. And I will listen to you. You will seek me and find me when you seek me with all your heart. And I will bring you back from captivity."

I sat in stunned disbelief. In an instant, I knew I had found a higher being I could trust. A God that is compassionate, loving, forgiving and wants the best for me. I decided that pivotal day to follow the Divine that created me and all of life's beauty in its likeness. I consider myself to be divinely and spiritually connected to our Creator, and I nurture that relationship every single day. I am committed to living a *spiritual* life outside the confines of many *religious* teachings.

I've been challenged many times about my Spiritual beliefs, mostly by Christians. Years ago, as a result of my childhood religious experiences, I embarked on a study of many religions and philosophies. I'm quite comfortable in proclaiming that I believe in many teachings, all rooted in the common denominator of Love. I have a loving and deeply profound connection with Jesus, the Buddha, Zen teachings, and many other Eastern philosophies and religions.

Most importantly, I now know and trust that I am cloaked in the love and grace of my Creator. It's where I find spiritual guidance and comfort, wrapped in undeniable, unconditional love. Whether we refer to our Creator as God, the Universe, Higher Power, or simply Love, matters not. We are all created in the likeness of eternal beauty, love, understanding, compassion, mercy and grace. We are as unique as our DNA. We are all doing the best we can to maneuver through this maze called Life. To suggest there is only one way to journey through it seems ludicrous to me.

There has been nothing more comforting to my Spirit than to hold to the universal truth of Love that was borne out of my fears, questions and uncertainty. I'm confident the unknowing - the questions, the uncertainty- is all part of the beauty of Faith. I don't know what happens when we die. I don't know if there is a heaven or hell. I've become comfortable with not *knowing*. My faith is in the beauty, renewal and resurrection that resides in each of us and in everything that surrounds us. That's enough for me, for now.

If your faith is faltering, welcome it as an opportunity to ask questions and seek guidance until you are yet again grounded in the Truth of Love that best serves you. If you are challenged by the well-meaning, main-stream suggestion, "There is only one way to God," simply nod, smile and respond, "Thank you for sharing." Then, go about your way of leaning into the comfort of your personal faith.

If you are not a faith-based person or you are struggling to find your way, simply wrap yourself in Grace. While most people associate Grace with religion, the dictionary offers a secular meaning as well. Here's my favorite:

Grace: To confer dignity, honor, mercy, kindness or compassion.

Let's think about what it would look like if we wrapped ourselves in the type of Grace that would allow for deep transformation.

For me, Grace can be found in the simplest of things. I love a warm drink, whether it be coffee or tea. Most mornings, I start with the intention of making the best cup of coffee I can make. I enjoy every sip that conjures up, "Oh yes, that's perfect!" It's the most delightful start to my day.

I also love the comfort of a big warm blanket, a sweatshirt, sweatpants, socks or slippers, my feet curled beneath my thighs as I lose myself in a good movie.

Proper rest and body movement allow me to *honor* what my body needs. I can cover myself with *compassion* when the ugly cry comes, and I can handle most anything with *dignity*, no matter my mood.

I am also keenly aware of allowing myself *mercy* when I make a mistake of any kind. There was a time when I would beat myself up if I made a mistake. No matter how small or large, I would badger and demean myself, having thoughts that no one else would have against me. We all know we can be our own worst enemy. Start paying attention to the way you demean yourself. Replace it with a dose of Grace.

Allow Grace to be a warm, soothing blanket over your soul. Curl up with it and allow it to cover you in kindness, mercy, dignity, compassion and honor. Then, pay it forward.

The Ocean is My Container

In my heart of hearts, I'm a beach bum. I'm a Pisces, so it resonates with my soul. I've taken many walks along many beaches, giving thanks and finding comfort. On a recent walk, while on a solo journey to the Outer Banks, I thought about how many times in my life I've given heartache over to the ocean. It just seems large enough to serve as a container for that which I cannot carry. It's always very cathartic for me to sit in the sand, pen to paper, and release my hurts and sorrows to something greater than myself.

The ocean has always served as solace for me. It holds all the hurts, all the despair, all the agony and all of the hope my heart can't hold in a given moment. Our grief can be a beautiful path to exposing the deepest part of ourselves that needs to be revealed and released in order to live the highest, most authentic version of ourselves. It can also be incredibly overwhelming and take up so much space we feel we can barely breathe.

I believe it's important we make room in our hearts for the revealing. It's not a matter of "getting over our pain" or "moving on." It's simply a means of creating space for the unknown yet welcome glimmers of hope for our future. While some can turn to their faith or God to hold these tender places, some feel lost in the unknowing. They simply may not have faith in something outside their hearts that can hold the magnitude of their grief.

Where can you deposit your heartache, pain and uncertainty in order to make room to explore the highest expression of your future? Take a moment to explore that question for yourself. If you don't know, nature is a good place to start. It is vast, wide and deep and serves as a reminder of the beauty in the circle of life. It is there, waiting for us to witness, observe and hold with reverence.

No matter what you determine your container to be, embrace it with both arms. Within it, you will find relief and release and a realization that there is something outside yourself that is strong and bold yet gentle enough to hold the gigantic boulder sitting squarely on your chest. Go ahead….give it away for now.

Choose The Right Hairapist

I don't know about you, but if my hair isn't right, *everything* else seems off kilter. When I need a haircut or highlight, I need it *today*! Not tomorrow, not next week, today!

I suffered with Covid hair following a prolonged bout of the dreaded illness. My hair thinned and grew in what Jon affectionately referred to as "crop circles." The first time he said it, I burst into tears. Later, I found it humorous. It was the perfect description of what looked like round circles of matted hair growing in every imaginable direction. It was very upsetting and frustrating. Jon would stand behind me, lifting the thinning curls gently with his fingers, lovingly trying to convince me it was getting better. I knew it wasn't.

I went through three hairstylists in two cities, trying to find one that knew what to do. I grew increasingly frustrated and downright disheartened when I heard, "I'm sorry, I don't know what to do with it." It became apparent to me when someone either didn't believe in Covid, had never heard of Covid hair, or simply didn't know what to do about it. It was one frustrating visit after another.

And then, I met Melissa. She has worked at the same shop in a small town for over 20 years. When I sat down in her chair for the first time, she took special care to listen to what I was saying. She was very quiet as she ran a comb through my hair, examining it as though she was searching for hidden clues. She stepped back, then stepped back in to comb it again. She didn't say a word. Then, with the confidence I needed to hear, she agreed. "You have Covid hair," she uttered matter-of-factly. I've never felt so relieved. All I needed was for someone to listen and understand. She did. We worked together for months as she continued to offer words of encouragement and the experience of her studies, understanding and belief to bring my hair back to life.

Along the way, Melissa and I became trusted friends. I love sitting in her chair. We solve all the world's problems in a matter of thirty minutes. We laugh loudly and unapologetically. We talk about the idiots in Washington, clients that make us crazy, her daughter's unrelenting illness, my journey through grief, and the dumb things people do and say. It's all food for fodder. Her chair has become a safe and welcoming place for me to bare my soul and underbelly.

I had burned through countless talking heads before I finally found my therapist, Roberta. I knew the minute I met her that she was the one. Roberta has lovingly held my hands over more than three decades, gently guiding me to believe I was worthy of unconditional love, all the while listening compassionately as I unraveled painful childhood experiences. She gently led me to understand how and why my self-esteem and confidence had been eroded by the abuse of my parents. She literally saved my soul. Following our work together, we became close friends, and we continue to share a mutually rewarding relationship today. I remain grateful for her love, compassion and belief in me.

My business/life coach, Stacy, has guided me to reach levels of success I never imagined possible. She taught me to value time, hold myself accountable, and to believe in myself instead of having to prove myself. She guided me through the annual ritual of journey mapping, which is a guided roadmap for reaching one's deepest desires, something I continue to practice today. That practice alone has resulted in success I only imagined possible. Stacy continues to remind me of my strengths, my value, and my worth as a person as I continue on the road less traveled.

Traci, my physical health coach, has patiently guided me through hours of teaching me the power of a deep breath and building strong bones. On days when I didn't think I could muster up the energy to go to lift 5 lbs, she continues to gently encourage and remind me that my super power lies in my core strength. I will forever be thankful to her for helping guide me to better health over the past few years.

My writing coach, Valley, has inspired and encouraged me to write - and keep writing - when I wanted to give up and had lost confidence in my ability. I've never known anyone who listens as intently as Valley. She creates a safe space for the vulnerable to share their hearts through putting pen to paper in an atmosphere of trust and respect, the likes of which I've never experienced.

My primary care physician, Erin, held my hands in hers and, with tears streaming down her face, convinced me I was going to be okay following severe PTSD and memory loss following Jon's death. She encouraged and fostered my belief in a spiritual approach to holistic health care. That's a rare find, one I'm eternally grateful for.

Do their credentials matter? Yes and no. We certainly need to make sure that our providers are well-trained and educated in their fields. But, honestly, their willingness to practice from their hearts and get down on the mat with reality is what matters most. As Michael J. Fox reminds us, "The people living with the condition are the experts."

I've worked with therapists, doctors and coaches who are well-educated but didn't seem to be connected on an emotional level. I prefer the latter. I've grown to appreciate that experience trumps education - *every single time.*

Choose your hairapist and all other trusted guides wisely. Take time to *interview* therapists, coaches, medical providers and hairstylists. If you are not satisfied with your current caretakers, seek new ones. After all, the success of your guided transformation is gently held in their loving, capable and transformative hands.

Barter for Healing

Think you don't have the resources to hire a therapist, life coach or personal trainer to help you achieve a life well lived? Think again. We all have unique talents, skills and commodities to offer or trade. You can put yours to work to help someone else, all the while investing in yourself!

I had just declared bankruptcy when I searched for a therapist during my second marriage. I had no idea how I was going to put food on the table or pay my monthly bills, much less hire a therapist. At the same time, I had a strong, burning desire in my Spirit to seek the help I needed to heal my fragile Spirit.

So, I sought the services of a therapist who was on staff at a local church. She was recommended to me by someone who was teaching a *free* Divorce Recovery Workshop. In our first meeting, I was honest and told her that I could not afford her services, nor did I have insurance to cover it. She simply smiled and nodded with unspoken understanding and acknowledgment. I asked if I could pay her in $10 installments towards her $50 hourly fee. I promised to pay her in full for as long as it took. She agreed, and it was never mentioned again.

A few years ago, I had a small office space for rent. A woman called in response to my ad and said that her business was growing, and she wanted to move her office outside her home. The minute she walked in the door, I knew I wanted to know her. Confident, beautiful and assured, she had something I desired, and I was intrigued. She told me about her business coaching practice. She explained how she helps women reach higher levels of achievement in their business and personal lives. The more she talked, the more I wanted to listen. I had floundered for years, one mistake after another, needing help I didn't want to ask for nor thought I could afford.

I'm not sure which one of us brought it up first, but we bartered her coaching services for my office space. Stacy became a very important person in my life, coaching me to heights I never dreamt possible for myself, including writing this book. I will be forever grateful she showed up and was willing to barter.

It takes committed willingness and practice to negotiate for what you want or need. Sometimes, our desires are met by the Universe, sometimes they are met by hard work, and sometimes they can be met by the exchange of resources.

Seek out the services you desire, and then make a list of the services you can offer. Can you clean someone's house in exchange for a massage? Can you mow someone's lawn in exchange for electrical services? Can you exchange counseling for accounting services? Anything can be bartered. After all, money is simply an exchange of energy. And energy is unlimited. It's simply waiting for you to tap into it.

Trust me, that's how the Universe really works.

Explore What Makes Your Heart Happy

Most heartache is the result of a significant life change. The death of a cherished loved one, a terminal or debilitating illness, a divorce or job loss can leave us feeling uncertain, bewildered and confused. Our future may look bleak, and we may feel lost in the wilderness. But there is a little spark deep inside that is waiting for us to fan its embers. Now may be the time to explore what truly makes your heart sing.

In "The Artist's Way: A Spiritual Path to Higher Creativity," Julia Cameron encourages us to take ourselves on a weekly date. I first took her course about eight years ago. It suggests you commit to writing three long-hand pages every day, followed by taking yourself on a weekly date - alone. The writing is cathartic, but I find the weekly dates to be more so. I have connected with various personal interests, including photography, writing, cooking, movies, travel adventures, and hiking, just to name a few. The opportunities are endless, and I've grown to explore things I never would have in the past.

I talk with plenty of people, primarily women, who share that they wish they could do things on their own but feel "afraid" to be alone. I get it. It can feel intimidating and scary. My suggestion is to start with something simple. You don't have to spend a lot of money or time to take yourself on a date. Take a book to a coffee shop and, sit in a corner and read for an hour, sipping on your favorite beverage. Go on a hike near your house. Enjoy nature, it's everywhere. Take a walk on the beach. Go to the library, a museum or an art gallery. Make some popcorn, curl up and watch a movie. Take a drive down a long and winding road, not knowing where it leads. Color outside the lines. Take a class that sparks your interest. Or simply fix yourself a nice meal, plate it on a lovely piece of art, and sit down and enjoy every bite.

Just a few months after Jon's death, I signed up for a writing workshop. I was totally intimidated and apprehensive. But, I learned that everyone else in the group seemed to be experiencing much of the same. Most everyone was in the process of unraveling something and also felt uncertain of their writing abilities. Often, the participants would offer an apology about their writing abilities prior to sharing what they had written.

As we listened to the unraveling of love affairs, marriages, concerns about children, uplifting stories of times past, or the loss of a loved one, it became apparent we had more in common than we thought. No one really cared about the writing itself. The class became a safe refuge for us to share our innermost thoughts and feelings. And I made a few new friends along the way. The writing workshops eventually led to writing this book - something I've longed to do most of my adult life but was never able to muster up the courage to do - until now.

Whatever interests you have, devote some time towards them. Make a commitment to explore new ones or reignite something that sets your heart on fire. It doesn't have to be a perfect match. You can start small as you feed your soul with thoughtful care.

Make a list of your top interests and make a date with yourself to explore them. Relax into the adventure!

Put Pen to Paper

It's a proven fact that unattended emotions travel through our bodies and land in vital organs. It doesn't take a rocket scientist to observe the damage we cause to our physical and emotional well-being by dismissing our deeply buried emotions. Heartache takes up residence in the deepest crevices of our souls, longing for a way to be heard and acknowledged. We can throw substances, food or pills at numbing it, or we can take the road less traveled to actually work towards a healthy healing of our pain. Taking pen to paper can be a useful tool towards that end.

I've been a "closet" writer most of my life. For decades, I kept my journals, boxes, and paper bags of writings under my bed and in my attic, never to see the light of day. Just a few years ago, when I was moving and was forced to clean out my attic, I dragged them out, dusted them off and sat in stunned silence as I read what I had written about my life experiences, hopes and dreams. My life was laid bare before me, and I found great comfort in reading what had spilled from my heart onto blank pages.

About four months prior to Jon's death, he asked me if I would write our love story. I shrugged and said, "Sure, one day." He stopped me, held my shoulders firmly and told me he was serious. He made it clear it was important to him. The next day, I drove to Barnes & Noble to find the perfect journal to hold our story. I searched and searched the bookshelves until the perfect one peeked out from the bottom shelf. It was light brown leather with a big, bold heart emblazoned on the front. There was a thin leather strap that wrapped around it twice to hold it closed. I knew immediately it was the one. I took it home and showed it to him with pride.

Sadly, the first time I wrote in it was a few months later, just days following his death. I used our sacred journal to write love letters to him every morning. It served me well to pour my grief onto those beautiful leather-bound pages he would never read. It brought me comfort to talk with him daily, to share my innermost thoughts and feelings, and to get them out of my system. It was cathartic and transforming.

You don't need to consider yourself a writer to jot your thoughts down. This is about freeing your heart and soul of the emotions, hopes, and dreams held hostage in the crevices. You may be surprised just how impactful and freeing it can be.

Make a date with yourself to find the perfect journal that will inspire you to privately record your innermost thoughts and feelings. Hold it in your hands. Run your fingers over its cover. Be sure it's the perfect one that will inspire you. After all, it's going to hold precious thoughts and the deepest desires for your future.

Slow Down for Yellow Lights

When we are in emotional turmoil, energy is our best friend. If we deplete it, we can find ourselves in deep trouble, fighting relentless fatigue and deeper depression. We must be diligent to protect our energy first and foremost. This is not easy in a culture that glorifies "busyness," but it is essential to our well-being.

I've been told countless times since Jon's death that I just need to "stay busy." I understand the theory, but it's not always the best advice. I believe we need to encourage more rest for the weary. After all, the roller coaster of emotion, the business we must attend to in the wake of endings, and our stark reality is exhausting enough without feeling the need to "stay busy!"

I've canceled more social events and outings than I care to admit over the past couple of years. I'd make the decision to agree to seemingly fun or potentially distracting plans one minute, only to regret it the next. I'd try to muster up the strength to keep a commitment, all the while dreading the exhaustion of it. I would try to convince myself that I could continue with the plans, all the while knowing deep down that it wasn't good timing and would lead to further anxiety and fatigue. I became so ashamed of canceling plans that I stopped making them. That's not healthy, either.

I decided to approach making plans with boundaries. I've learned to tell family and friends up front that I am still vulnerable and on shaky ground. I warn them that I may have to decline plans at the last minute. This way, I don't have to feel guilty if I'm not able to muster up the strength to get out of my pajamas. I've already established the possibility.

I recently declined an invitation to an annual holiday party, one I've attended ritually for years. When asked why I would not be attending, I responded by saying, "I'm conserving my energy." That night, I stayed home, curled up under a cozy blanket, had a glass of wine and watched a movie. It was energy-restoring, and I felt good about my decision. I was taking care of myself.

People are generally understanding and appreciative when I share my vulnerability. After all, that's really where our strength lies. When shared, it creates a safe space between loved ones to communicate authentically.

Be gentle with yourself while re-engaging socially. You will find yourself gaining in strength and energy to engage socially as your healing progresses. It may take some time and even a few seemingly failed attempts, but it will happen. In the meantime, practice saying, "No, thank you," and let it be enough. It's an empowering gift to yourself you won't regret. The people who love you will understand. And as you gain strength, you will know when the time's right to venture out and authentically enjoy yourself.

Be gentle with yourself as you lean into a deep breath as you embrace the healing process. After all, as LE Bowman writes, "It isn't the strike that hurts; it's the surviving. The cut of the shards the first breath after. The realizing that through all the pain, you must somehow learn how to breathe again." Oh, the sacred art of breathing again.

The Ugly Cry

Life doesn't seem to care about our heartache. We are encouraged at every turn to "get up and move on." We have babies to feed, work to be done so we can pay the bills that are stacking up, houses to clean and groceries to buy. The demands of life are relentless and no more profound than when our hearts are shattered on the floor before us.

I wish we took a different approach as a culture to those who are suffering through the day as a result of life's demands. We could take beautiful cues from our friends in other parts of the world who dress in black for a year, sit Shiva, or deliver meals for a prolonged period of time. Perhaps we need Life Managers who step in to pay bills, change diapers, grocery shop and the like until the bereaved can get their shit together.

When we are in deep grief, we don't know how we are going to get out of bed, much less face the demands of the world. We put on our fake faces, smile and nod, and pretend to be okay when someone dares to ask how we are doing. It takes a tremendous amount of energy to face the world and all its requirements. All along, we are shoring up the inevitable. The ugly cry.

As ridiculous as it may sound, sometimes you may need to schedule a cathartic cry. That's right, put it on your calendar!

I remember thinking, "If I can get through my workday, I can go home and cry at 5:30." I would make it my goal to just get to 5:30. And sometimes it worked.

Just recently, I found myself in a surprising state of unexpected grief. I had been going along, doing well, and then whammy! As the holidays were approaching, I began to feel overwhelmed, over-tired and over-scheduled. I was incredibly busy planning an annual holiday business party, planning Thanksgiving dinner in another town, and helping plan my oldest son's wedding celebration that would follow the Saturday after Thanksgiving. Whew, just writing about it makes me anxious and fatigued.

I could feel the ugly cry building up with a vengeance. I didn't have time or energy for it that particular week, so I scheduled it for the following Monday. Oh boy, was it ugly. But it was the release I needed. Amazingly enough, the scheduling of an ugly cry gives me something to look forward to. It's a much-needed release, and I know it's going to feel so damn good!

There will be times when you just can't keep the tears from flowing while you are in the grocery store or, at your work desk or driving in your car. Just recently, I was in Trader Joe's, buying wine for a holiday party. There were too many people crammed into my aisle. I felt the "walls" closing in. I had a total meltdown right there on the *"whine"* aisle. I sobbed right through the checkout line and into my car. That's okay too!

It is my experience that the release we gain from a good solid cry can create space for other things, such as peace and inspiration. It's good for our souls. Don't let anyone shame you into "bucking up" from a good, much needed, understandable and deserved sobbing session!

If you are not a crier, that's okay too. It is, however, important that you find ways to release the pent-up emotions that come from not relinquishing them. Use a pillow as a punching bag. Go slam some tennis balls or baseballs.

Whatever you can do to release emotions of frustration, anger, disappointment and sadness will make you feel better.

Go ahead. Put a good cry or a session with a punching bag on your calendar. You'll be relieved you did.

Magic Erasers

Can we please take a magic eraser to holidays and anniversaries? When we are tending broken hearts, nothing seems more cruel than to have to face a holiday or anniversary. The "first" of all things can conjure up emotions we never imagined. Whether we are facing the onslaught of holidays, the first anniversary following the end of a marriage, or the dreaded date of the first anniversary of a death, it can be brutal and overwhelming.

Holidays seem worse, I believe, because of the cultural message of their importance. We put so much emphasis on holidays that it's hard to escape them. I'm all for spending time with family and friends. I remain fond of several holidays, Thanksgiving being my favorite. I'm also in favor of skipping them if we simply can't conjure up the energy or desire to see them through.

There have been days I simply wanted to scream, "Can we please cancel this date on the calendar?" "Will the world come to an end if I simply can't show up for Christmas?" Grieving can be tough enough without the added pressure of having to face days that bring dread just by the flip of a calendar page.

I have learned to create new and welcoming ways to honor and celebrate certain days. Just recently, when faced with what would have been mine and Jon's anniversary, I decided to honor it by purchasing a lovely, heart-shaped locket that will hold his ashes close to my heart forever.

One of the best Christmases I've ever enjoyed was spent with two girlfriends on the island of Turks and Caicos. We sunbathed, drank margaritas and wrote Merry Christmas in the sand. None of us visited with family that day, but we look back on that holiday vacation and declare it was filled with fun, love, laughter and peaceful celebration.

Last year, when facing mine and Jon's birthdays, which are just three days apart, I took a trip to Fort Myers, Florida, to volunteer to help victims of a major hurricane. Looking back, I can't think of another way I would have wanted to celebrate and honor the day of his birth. I felt he was right there, by my side, swinging a hammer and consoling people who had lost all of their personal belongings. It was good for my soul.

When a friend was facing her son's birth date following his unexpected death, I encouraged her to find a way to celebrate his life in a rich and meaningful way. She elected to have a picnic lunch in a particular waterfront park she enjoys. She made a delicious meal, complete with birthday cake, and enjoyed some time alone in contemplation and in honor of her beloved son. She plans to do the same next year.

On the first anniversary of Jon's death, which was also my son and daughter-in-law's first wedding anniversary, the day fell on Easter Sunday. It felt like a triple whammy. For weeks prior, the dread of it was palpable amongst our entire family. At first, we simply didn't know what to do. Should we ignore it and let it pass? Should we cry and scream in agony? Or should we celebrate it and let it have its way with us, whatever that entails? We chose the latter.

We agreed to attend church together as a family. We cried all the way through it. Then, we gathered at a brewery that happened to have outdoor games and firepits. Both of my sons, their wives, and all of my grandchildren gathered for an afternoon of *celebration*. My oldest son gifted a hand-crafted clock to his brother. He etched into the wood, "On Edgar Time," with the date of his wedding. On the back, he burned into the wood, "In loving memory of Jon Seavey." We laughed and cried. And we agreed to do it again next year.

Grief is designed to be communal. Unfortunately, we have not quite found our way back to the sacred rituals that are so important in helping us move through heartache as a result of Covid. If we can't find our way back to the vital importance of communal gatherings, we can develop new rituals that can help foster healing within our brokenness.

We can reframe holidays, anniversaries and other special occasions by creating new, rich and deeply meaningful rituals. Take some time to think about how you would like to spend your next holiday or anniversary in a way that will bring comfort to your heart. Or, if you prefer, grant yourself the gift of skipping it.

It's Okay to Not Feel Grateful

All The Freaking Time

We glorify gratitude as much, if not more, than staying busy. I'm not suggesting gratefulness is not important. Of course, it is. But it should not overshadow the reality of deep loss or a broken heart *in the moment.* There is a time to feel deep and authentic gratitude, and there is a time to sit with the worst of our feelings. Sometimes, the only way out is through.

Our culture is bent towards spiritual and emotional bypassing. It is strongly suggested that if we feel grateful enough or spiritual enough, our pain will magically disappear. It doesn't. It gets buried beneath the surface of superficial gratitude for our culture's sake. It's the same message as "stay busy," "be strong," "get up and go." Just "be grateful." Believe me, it's not healthy.

If you are struggling to feel gratitude within your heartache, that's normal - and it's okay. Take a deep breath. Don't feel pressured to dismiss your natural and normal feelings to that of superficial gratitude. Be reminded two things can be true at the same time. I can feel grateful for my two sons, all the while grieving my unborn baby and the loss of never being able to have another. I can feel grateful to have met and enjoyed a committed and loving relationship with Jon, and still want to puke my guts out and rage in anger over his tragic and untimely death. We can grieve as long as we need to grieve or feel what we need to feel and then be thankful when *authentic* gratitude shows up.

I brace myself when someone says, "Be grateful for the wonderful memories you have," or "Look on the bright side and count your blessings," as though platitudes of gratefulness should somehow magically wash away the deep rage, confusion and despair I may be *feeling* in a particular moment. We can't afford to trick ourselves into feeling grateful. If we do, our pain will live below the surface, lying in wait to erupt for the rest of our lives.

You don't have to look too far or listen too intently to get the message we should just be grateful. It comes from pulpits, advertisements, and social influencers. I've started countless Grateful Journals, only to fill other journals with what is truly troubling my soul. Don't get me wrong. I give thanks every day. I know how fortunate and blessed I am, and I know there is always something to be grateful for. And

I cherish those moments with true and authentic reverence. At the same time, I refuse to overshadow my heartache with superficial gratitude.

Don't be rushed or shamed into feeling grateful. You don't have to find the positive in every situation. Sometimes awful, heart-wrenching things happen, and it's okay to see it for what it is. Let it have its way. Your heart is hurting and you deserve to move through that pain at your own pace, in your own time. With the healthy release of rage, heartache and despair, pain is unleashed in magnitude, ultimately allowing gratefulness to take its rightful place at the right time.

Embrace gratitude when it's authentic, and rejoice in the unleashing of your heartache when the time is right.

And always remember: Two things can be true at once.

The Veil Is Thin

While preparing to write this chapter, I stumbled upon an article written by a well-known, doctorate-holding Biblical scholar. She completely debunks the idea that our loved ones communicate with us following death. Instead, she proclaims with certainty that we are assigned angels appointed by God to comfort us in our grief. Part of God's kingdom, these angels are assigned to comfort and guide, but they most certainly are not our loved ones. Well, okay then. I'm not one to put up a religious argument, especially to a Biblical *scholar*, but I will offer a Spiritual one based on experience.

Not long after my brother died, when I was just 14, I began to have a repetitive dream for months following his death. I was riding a school bus, and when I arrived home, there was a large gathering of people in the front yard. I was too short to see over the heights of all the adults, so I had to push my way through. Imagine my disbelief and delight when I made my way to the center of the gathering to see my brother, who was being welcomed home. It was so real that I looked forward to going to sleep every night, anticipating his visit. It comforted me just to see him in my dreams and to feel the sense of his loving presence. I believed he was visiting me to let me know he was still present.

After Jon's death, I was overwhelmed by the reality of loss, panic and utter shock. Because he died suddenly and without warning, I found myself in a daze of undeniable despair and confusion. I simply wanted to talk with him and hear his voice. I needed to know he was close by. I started asking him for bold and magnificent signs to confirm he was. He didn't disappoint.

I can't count the number of times I asked for something specific to happen, and within days, if not hours, it would. Requested flowers were delivered randomly. He spoke to me directly and with intention when I asked for his guidance. He appeared to my five-year-old grandson numerous times with specific and profound messages. Butterflies and cardinals became frequent visitors, in numbers never experienced in my life.

One day, when I was traveling alone to Colonial Beach to escape the madness of having to make some tough decisions about where I was going to live in the wake of Jon's death, his voice directed me to take a walk down by the waterside. I argued, saying I was tired and wanted to stay inside. His voice kept nudging me. Reluctantly and with a little irritation, I gathered my coat and shoes and headed down to the park bench as he had instructed. I waited and waited for a sign, but it didn't come in the ten minutes I was willing to sit there. I thought, "This is ridiculous; you have completely lost your mind."

Just then, I noticed vultures fighting over a carcass on the beach. I watched for a while and wondered if that could possibly be some sort of message. I dismissed it. I waited for a cardinal or butterfly to visit. No such luck. I grew impatient, stood up, and thought, "That's it. I've had enough." Jon's voice spoke again. "Have some patience, Woman," I couldn't ignore his request, especially when he was calling me by his favorite nickname.

A few minutes later, I caught a glimpse of a tiny little seagull floating out in the water, probably 100 feet offshore. It was bobbing up and down, riding the waves easily and without effort. It rode the waves all the way into shore. Its little legs touched down, and it began leisurely walking the beach, pecking food from the sand along the way. After a while, it rode the waves back out to sea, finally taking a solo flight out of my sight.

In the meantime, the vultures were still fighting. There they were, pecking each other almost to death while devouring the carcass as though it may be their last meal. I found the contrast to be ironic. And then, Jon's voice came back into my head. "Pick one. Be the vulture or be the seagull." I chose the latter. In that moment, I was able to make a decision about how I was going to live in the wake of turmoil following his death.

The next day, I went back to the beach and took a picture of the park bench. I sent it to an artist friend of mine and told her the story. A few months later, she showed up at my door with a painting of the park bench facing the waterfront. It hangs on my bedroom wall as a morning reminder of how I choose to live my life.

Just recently, a dear friend called me in tears to let me know that her son had sent her a sign from heaven. It was her granddaughter's birthday, and while speaking with her on the phone, her Ring doorbell chimed, letting her know there was someone at the front door. This time, it was two cardinals, male and female. A sign from above when she needed it most. I was so happy and excited for her. We literally cried together in celebration.

Often, when sharing these stories with friends and family, I get the stare as though I have two heads. You know, the look, the tipping of the head, the raising of the eyebrows, and the rehearsed response, "*That's interesting.*" Then, there are those who believe. They offer comfort in confirmation. They welcome hearing about every encounter and every message. And they celebrate the moments with me.

I'm not sure what the fear is surrounding signs and wonders or visits from the departed. We have enjoyed a deeply profound and loving relationship with our loved ones while they are here on earth - hence the depth of our grief. If we are spiritually connected on earth, it seems reasonable our spiritual connection continues through eternity. I prefer to believe they continue to communicate and guide us because of that deep, eternal connection. If you believe in signs and wonders, keep believing. Don't allow anyone to try to convince you otherwise!

Let's Refrain From Comparing Heartache

I believe our culture feels the need to compare heartache because everyone is screaming for their pain to be seen and heard. Sadly, in order for our pain to be acknowledged within our society, we feel the need to wave a flag of ours "being the worst." If we collectively shifted how we deal with heartache and gave it its proper attention, we would not have the need or desire to compare it. My pain is my pain, and yours is yours. We really have no right to claim one being greater than another.

I've often heard the death of a child is "the worst" pain anyone can experience. I can't speak to that because I've never experienced it. What I do know is that the pain of losing anyone we have loved deeply or had a soulful connection with can be debilitating, isolating and completely overwhelming. It can throw us off course, off center, and into the throws of the most difficult transformation we will ever experience. The same can be said for many other heart-wrenching and life-changing experiences.

Now, before anyone gets their panties in a twist, let me be clear. Not all pain is the same. No two tragedies are alike, nor should they be considered so. I understand there is a "hierarchy" of tragedy. The pain associated with a divorce is very different from the death of a partner, spouse or child. Losing a job doesn't bring on the same amount of heartache that the suffering over the loss of a loved one might, nor should it. Of course, the loss of a child is devastating and most likely tagged "the worst" because it's completely out of *natural order*. That alone elevates that type of loss to a level that many of us will never understand without the experience of it. It may very well deserve a category of its own.

Still, heartache should not be compared for the simple sake of comparison. There is plenty of room for everyone's pain *if* we strive to honor it properly and with collective compassion.

I've often heard people say, "My trauma doesn't compare to yours," or "My pain is not as great as yours," or "You would never understand my pain." The latter statement is most likely true. None of us can truly know the pain of another. We can empathize and imagine, but we will *never* know how another person truly feels. Not ever. Let's stop suggesting that we do.

What I do know is that the diminishing of our pain, or that of another over ours, doesn't serve a healthy purpose. Let's start from the premise that it all sucks and requires a great deal of empathy, energy, time, patience, understanding and compassion. Deep, life-changing, heart-altering woundedness should never be compared.

Let's begin by honoring the pain we see in the hearts of one another, no matter the reason or circumstance. In doing so, we will create space for vulnerability and a safe place for being heard, followed by ultimate and sanctified transformation. Let's be gentle with our collective grieving. Together, we can generate a cultural shift to hold sacred that which deserves honor between us.

You Haven't Lost Your Sense of Humor

It's Just Temporarily Buried Under The Rubble

For almost two years after Jon died, I thought my sense of humor had been banished to hell. Seriously. I truly feared it was lost forever.

Humor has always been important to me. I found solace in it when I was a kid, and I still do. I would pretend I was on stage, making people laugh. I sat in anticipation of a good belly laugh as I watched Johnny Carson, Robin Williams and many other talented souls bring smiles and laughter to the world. I learned early on that humor served a cathartic purpose. I believed in the adage, "laughter is the best medicine," and I still do.

During deeply challenging times, it hasn't been laughter that pulled me through. In fact, very little seemed humorous to me. I wondered how others could find humor in anything while I was curled in a fetal position on the floor. Instead, I looked to trusted counselors, my therapist, my spiritual beliefs and countless self-development books to carry me through. While that served the greater purpose at the time, I longed for my belly to roar and tears to stream down my face from laughing so damn hard. In the depths of grief, it simply wouldn't come.

I shared with my writing coach, Valley, that I was actually terrified my sense of humor would never return following Jon's death. She assured me it would. Little by little, it began to show up in my writing. There it was, peeking its head out from the crevices of despair. Little snippets of laughter and light-heartedness. It was there, buried deep in the darkness, just waiting for light to wake it up and bring life to it again.

The worst of our days don't always leave much room for humor. In fact, there is a part of us that may feel guilty for desiring it. The phenomenon of survivor's guilt, for example, is real. Too real. It's absurd, really, to think that the death of someone else should make us feel guilty for living. But there it is.

The questions come into our consciousness as truth. How could you possibly laugh or have fun right now? Isn't that some sort of sacrilege? Sadly, the answer is too often a resounding "Yes!" And, so we wait. We simply hope our sense of humor will return before we succumb to what I call the procession of the living dead.

There will be days when you will feel lighthearted, and laughter may come more easily. There will also be days when you don't think anything is funny, and you may even resent others who simply suggest you "just need to lighten up." Welcome the days when you can laugh and find solace in humor. And honor the days when you can't. It's all grist for the mill.

I promise your sense of humor will return. Just be patient with it. As your healing progresses, so will your ability to laugh and find humor in the simplest of things. For now, take comfort in knowing it's not lost forever. It's just hidden under the rubble, waiting and longing with you.

What Are You Waiting For?

We live in a "microwave" society. We want everything *now*. If only we could be healed *now*. If only this pain would stop *now*. As in instantly. If only we didn't have to wait for the heartache to subside. If only…..

Sadly, transformation doesn't work that way. True healing requires a lot of patience and energy. And, unfortunately, waiting is a crucial part of it. We may be waiting for someone to make a decision before we can make one. We may be waiting for test results. We may be waiting for someone to accept our apology. We may be waiting for money to pay our bills. We may be waiting for someone to pass away. We may be waiting to find the right therapist or the funds to pay for one. We may be waiting for someone to agree to sign divorce papers. We may be waiting to feel better or waiting for the perfect time to move or write a book. We may be waiting for the new job offer to come through. We often spend a lot of time *waiting*.

Sometimes waiting is born of necessity, sometimes it's a response to our own fear of the future. Regardless of the reason, we must get comfortable with it. If we do, it can become our friend, and we can find comfort or opportunity in it. If we don't, it can serve as frustration and prolonged heartache.

Perhaps it's what we do while we are waiting that truly matters. Recently, I was sitting in my doctor's office waiting for a scheduled appointment. The doctor was running behind schedule. I elected to read while I was waiting. I didn't become frustrated or upset by the inconvenience. When the nurse called my name and suggested she was sorry they kept me waiting, I responded, "I wasn't waiting. I was reading." She laughed and said that was the first time a patient had responded in that manner.

The same principle can be applied to waiting while we are healing. While we wait for the broken pieces of our heart to mend, we can take a deep breath and realize that waiting, too, is simply part of the process. The old adage, "Good things come to those who wait," may apply here. That's not to say it's easy. Sometimes, most times, waiting is frustrating and annoying at best. But we can learn to embrace it with anticipation, wonder and grace.

Get comfortable with waiting. While you are waiting for an answer or a perfect time to do something or waiting for something to "come through," do something else. Time is too valuable to spend it wishing and wasting it away. Wait with purpose and put it to work for you. You may be surprised by the outcome.

Be gentle with yourself during this crucial time of waiting, and remember that sometimes it is vital for your overall well-being.

Someone You Know Needs Your Help

When I'm emotionally or physically depleted, the last thing I have the energy or goodwill to do is something for someone else. After all, heartache demands most of our attention. It's designed that way. Oftentimes, we find ourselves feeling exhausted, worn down and incapable. Who has the energy to do something for someone else when we can barely muster the energy to brush our own teeth?

Many of my friends are always doing something for someone else. I watch in amazement as they are always delivering meals, sending notes, giving generously and meeting the personal needs of others. It's a beautiful thing and something I aspire to. During my healing process I took cues from my friends and loved ones who do a better job than I of serving the hurting hearts and needs of others.

Just eleven months following Jon's death, I took a huge leap of faith and volunteered to go to Ft. Myers, Florida, to assist the victims of a major hurricane. I wanted to do something to celebrate our birthdays, which are three days apart in early March. I'm not sure what provided the energy or stamina for me to make the trip so soon after his death, but I did it. I could have just as easily gone to a deserted island to soothe my breaking heart, but I elected instead to do something bigger than myself to distract me from the impending meltdown I was certain to experience.

I was one of the oldest of 46 volunteers, all housed and sleeping in the same room on army cots for a week. We ate all of our meals together and shared two bathrooms and two showers. The moment I arrived, I thought to myself, "What the hell have I done?" It turned out to be one of the most rewarding and satisfying things I've ever experienced in my life.

I made instant friends with people from all over the world. We helped a total of six families in as many days. Eight months following the hurricane, they were still without water or electricity. Think about that for a moment. Eight months later. Right here, in the good ole USA. How could this be? I met wonderful people who had lost everything except the clothes on their backs.

Their dripping, wet, moldy and mildewed clothes and furnishings were piled up in their front yards. The stench was something I will never forget. Yet, they were full of gratitude and hope. They provided me with hope. I knew if they could get through the grief of losing everything they owned, I could get through mine.

I have learned serving others also serves as a healing balm for our hurting hearts. Every time I pick up the phone to check on someone, or deliver a note, or sit with someone who just needs to be heard, I have contributed to their healing, and I feel better. It's really that simple. So, in helping someone else, I've also taken a step towards healing my heartache. I've learned that being vulnerable allows others to do the same. And it opens the door to sharing our heartaches.

As hard as it may be, do something for someone else. Make a call, meet someone for lunch, take flowers to a neighbor, or volunteer. You will be pleasantly surprised how one small act of kindness towards another will bring you the greater gift of hope and blessings beyond measure. That's a win-win for everyone.

The Wake After The Wake

A major life-changing event can change *everything.* Your day-to-day routine is no longer. You may have to move. Your finances may be in shambles. There are arrangements to be made, claims to be filed, lawyers to consult. All the while, you are wondering how you will simply put one foot in front of the other. Your life is turned upside down, and your heart is broken. Nothing seems to conjure up more despair than what is required in the wake of death.

My friend, Debbie, spent the last decade managing a funeral home. The one thing she shared, time and again, is how sad it is when families are not prepared for the death of a loved one. And she's not referring to the emotional preparedness of a loss.

Sadly, more often than not, she met with families that had never discussed pre-arrangements. Many of them didn't even have a will. In some cases, she had to stand by helplessly as people didn't even have the legal right to claim the body of a loved one. Over and over, she watched in sadness as families were ripped apart as a result of lack of planning and expectations not being met. All because no one took the time to plan for the unthinkable.

As Jon and I were driving to my son's wedding in another state, just days before his death, we were finalizing our notes to revise our individual wills and trusts to include one another. Sadly, that didn't happen. We had agreed verbally what would happen if either of us died, but, unfortunately, our wishes didn't make it to a *legal* agreement. In an instant, I was living in our home, but it was not my house. I had to make the excruciating decision to move just months following his death.

I implore you. If you do not have your legal affairs in order, drop everything you are doing right now and make an appointment with an attorney. Seriously. Unless you have been through it, it's hard to imagine the nightmare your loved ones may face as a result. It's enough that they are having to deal with a loss of such magnitude. Please don't put them in the position of having to take care of your affairs as well.

As you move through the wake after the wake, you will be faced with what to do with personal belongings, whether to move or not, sorting out finances and the like. Take your time to make the tough decisions that come along with your life being turned upside down. Don't allow anyone to rush your decisions, no matter how small or insignificant they may seem.

While many will advise you not to make any major life decisions the first year following a significant event, oftentimes, that's simply not possible. Sometimes tough, challenging and downright stressful and difficult decisions must be made immediately. Trust yourself to make the necessary ones and leave the others for another day.

Take a deep breath, seek trusted counsel as you make your way, and be gentle with yourself through the process of rebuilding your life.

The Path Forward

While trying to write a "final chapter," it became clear to me that I couldn't. I could continue to write about the healing process forever. That's because that's what it is. A *process.* There is no period - the end - to authentic healing. Healing is not a destination. It is a journey. There is only the ebb and flow, to and fro, from one deep breath to the next, as we make our way to creating and living a *different* life.

It was just this past week, 22 months following Jon's death that I was able to read the hundreds of cards and letters I received upon his death. They sat in a box on my desk, in view, just waiting for me to be in the place of being able to receive them in a gracious, loving and reverent manner. I lit a candle and read every single one. Smiles came and tears flowed. I was so thankful I had waited for the right time to be present to fully receive the beautiful messages they contained. I was filled with compassion, reverence and joy, 22 months later.

Grief is an *active* process. It is love and your strength is in allowing it. Healing is hard work. Heart work is hard work. There will be questions that can't be answered, beliefs that will be challenged, days that will be cloaked in darkness, others that will be illuminated by hope and certainly by grace. It's all part of the journey.

With love and compassion for ourselves, the honoring of the aches of our hearts, and a commitment to continue to seek our deepest desires, we can take baby steps to awaken the healing process. We can begin to create authentic, joyful and fulfilling lives while also honoring our loved ones and life's challenging experiences as we begin to live *forward.*

In lieu of a "final chapter," I'd like to share the following poem with you. Written by my dear friend and writing coach, Valley Haggard, it hangs above my writing desk as a reminder to be gentle with myself and to hold tightly to the deepest desires of my heart.

I believe it offers a gentle way forward. It's shared with lots of love, compassion, hope and grace for your healing heart.

It's appropriately titled, "*Surrender Your Weapons.*"

"May you bring forth what is within you

May you walk through the fire of your stories

May you swim through the ocean of your words

May you dive bravely into the water of your memories

May you build the house of your body

May you write the story of your life

May you tell the stories that gut you, heal you

May you surrender to the process

May you trust what comes

May you go deeper into your life, into the truth,

than you've ever gone before

May you surface from the wreckage with rubies and stories and emeralds and gold

May you let sand and salt scrub you clean

May you follow your own thread to the end

May you be your own heroine, hero, warrior and muse

May you surrender your weapons

May you trust what comes."

My friend, the world needs your healed heart, with all its jagged and sharpened edges beautifully and lovingly pieced together. You are on the path to a life well lived, full of wonder, desire, bravery and courage, all the while honoring the hurts you will now gently carry with grace. You can do this, one sacred step at a time.

Above all else, please be gentle with yourself along the way.

Namaste.